GOING TO CHURCH IN THE FIRST CENTURY

BY ROBERT BANKS

AN EYEWITNESS ACCOUNT

GOING TO CHURCH IN THE FIRST CENTURY

BY ROBERT BANKS

Illustrations by
Judith Clingan

CHRISTIAN BOOKS
Publishing House

Auburn, Maine

copyright by
Robert Banks
1980
Printed in the
United States of America
by
Christian Books
Publishing House
Auburn, Maine

This book was originally published in 1980 by
Hexagon Press, Box 1302 Parramatta, NSW,
Australia 2150. Publishing rights were re-
assigned to Christian Books Publishing House
in 1990.

Banks, Robert John, 1939
National Library of Australia
Cataloguing-in-Publication Data

Illustrated by Judith Clingan
ISBN 0-940232-37-5

PREFACE

PREFACE

This brief narrative attempts to depict what it was like to attend an early christian gathering in the middle of the first century. Rome was chosen as the location because we know more about details of ordinary life there at that time than anywhere else. Aquila and Prisca were selected as hosts of the church because their long-term connection with Paul meant that the gathering in their home would most probably follow the line his letters suggest. As far as possible I have tried to base my portrait on data of one kind or another. Where there were gaps I had to speculate but have tried to do this in a controlled and non-arbitrary way.

The material utilised in this study came from biblical and other literary sources, both Roman and Greek, and from archaeological and inscriptional evidence. Much of it follows from a full-length study of *Paul's Idea of Community: The Early Housechurches in their Historical Setting* (Anzea, Sydney 1979), which was written over a number of years at Macquarie University, Sydney, Australia. Those who wish to see the scriptural basis that underlies the view of church presented in this booklet will be able to do so there. Research of the remainder of the material, particularly that connected with life in Rome in the first century, was undertaken during a sabbatical term at the University of Tubingen in South Germany. The help given by the Institute for the Study of Christian Origins made the task an easy and pleasant one.

In preparing the story, I received help from a number of people whom I would like to thank: the members of the Christliche Gemeinde in Tubingen, especially Scott Bartchy, for their hospitality during its preparation; Edwin Judge and Tom Hillard of Macquarie University, Sydney, for checking its historical accuracy; Liz and Peter Yuile, of Canberra, for reading the proofs; Clive and Ruth Monty, Jan Rolph and Humphrey Babbage of Canberra and Sydney respectively, for framing the accompanying discussion questions; and finally Ken Rolph, of Hexagon Press, Sydney, for his initial encouragement, helpful comments and editorial enterprise.

In issuing this, my only hope is that, whatever its inadequacies, christians may glimpse something here of what church once was, and still can be, like. We have lost something vital in the twenty centuries since. And even though we can't go back and simply imitate what the earliest christians did, the essential character of their meeting can be given appropriate twentieth century expression. That would involve many changes in our way of doing things today, but the gain would be immeasurable. In particular I have in mind those christians who have given up on church and for those searching individuals who are not christians at all. I hope they will find here a clearer idea of what they are looking for and ultimately that, like me, they may actually week by week experience it. To the many small groups of people throughout the world for whom these things are already true, this little story is dedicated.

PREFACE TO THE SECOND EDITION

It is gratifying to see this little booklet being reprinted. Over the last four years I have observed its use in a number of different contexts, e.g., theological and untheological, clerical and lay, adult and youth, congregational and educational. In each case it seems to have generated discussion at the level appropriate to those present. It has even been adapted dramatically for performance, again with considerable success. It has clearly enabled some people to sense the difference between early christian worship and much of our own in a way that mere exegesis or exposition has failed to do. We have followed Jesus' practice of story-telling too little in our attempts at christian communication.

As I re-read the story I am only too aware of its literary inadequacies. When I first conceived the idea I had hoped that someone more accomplished than I would be prepared to take the data I had assembled and write it up. I know that some people have found theological inadequacies in the story as well. While it is disputable, for example, that an outsider could be present at the Lord's Meal, I cannot myself see how such a person could in other ways participate in the meeting (1 Corinthians 14: 16, 24-25) yet be excluded from it without breaching laws of hospitality and denying them the possibility of a visual declaration of the gospel. On the basis of Passover precedent, I have no doubt about the presence of children. Others have questioned the comparative informality of the meal and of the service as a whole. Perhaps Jesus' words of institution were always quoted before the meal but I'm not certain that Paul's reference to them in 1 Corinthians 11 necessitates this, especially in view of the different versions we have of them in the gospels. Perhaps, too, greater formality reigned in the meetings generally, though the description of the gathering at Troas in Acts 20 would scarcely suggest this.

The new format of the booklet, for which thanks go to Ken Rolph of Hexagon Press, considerably enhances the story and, as before, Judy Clingan's elegant drawings continue to add life to the text.

Robert Banks

I, Publius

My name is Publius — Publius Valerius Amicius Rufus if you want to be exact. I come from Philippi, a comparatively new colony in Macedonia, one I am proud to say that is Roman through and through for all that it stands on Macedonian soil. At present I'm staying for a while with some old acquaintances of mine, Clement and Euodia, in Rome. Earlier today we all went out to dinner at a home nearby, and it was such a strange experience that I want to tell you about it. You see, my friends have a standing invitation from a Jewish couple called Aquila and Prisca to join with them every seventh day for a meal. This includes visitors as well, so I didn't need a special invitation to attend.

It was around mid-afternoon when we set out, well into the ninth hour of the day. In Rome, too, the main meal is generally eaten later in summer, especially when guests are included. I must say I found the narrow streets oppressive after being so long on the open road. Some of them were scarcely three metres wide. They were also muddy beyond description and quite insecure underfoot. Since work had already stopped for most, a fair number of people were already about, and at times we found it difficult to make our way. The streets wound so much, first this way, then that, that I soon lost whatever small sense of direction I had. It was just as well I didn't have to find the place we were going to myself. Most of the buildings don't have numbers, and few of the streets even have signs, so a stranger would be hard put to find his way.

The city's got so big. There must be well over a million people here now and it's growing all the

We went out to dinner — a strange experience

time. I doubt if there's a foreign country anywhere in the world that isn't represented here by a sizeable ethnic community. The Jews alone are said to number fifty thousand. Who was it who said that Rome wasn't one city any more but rather a conglomeration of cities, each with its own language, customs and occupations? It's been good for the economy, I suppose, for many of them have brought in skills which were in short supply among the local residents. The large inflow of slaves and freedmen has also alleviated the employment problem, though now it's become something of a burden. The food has improved too; there's so much more variety these days. But from a cultural point of view it's all a bit of a shambles. I prefer the way it used to be in earlier times. The good old days really were the best.

From a cultural point of view it's all a bit of a shambles

The street in which Aquila and Prisca lived, like most others in Rome, contained a mixture of housing styles. Once it had been full of small shops selling various kinds of goods, their owners either living at the rear of the premises or in pokey garrets above them. Then, during Tiberius' reign, a fire had burnt most of them to the ground. Once started in these wood and rubble buildings, a fire was hard to get under control. The few buildings that survived now stood beside towering blocks of tenements, some five or six storeys high. An even bigger fire risk, I'd have thought, quite apart from the constant risk of collapse, so badly built were many of the structures.

These high rise buildings are going up all over Rome, as they have been for decades. The great majority of people still live in this type of accom-

8

modation. Some of the more expensive ones, made out of brick and concrete, even come complete with new-fangled shopping arcades on the ground floor!

In one corner of the block were two free-standing houses. Not like those palatial mansions you see up on the hills around the city, but comfortable looking places all the same. Clement explained that the more imposing of the two was still in private hands. It had belonged to the same family for generations and the present owners had refused any number of lucrative offers to sell out so that it could be converted into apartments or turned into a boarding house. I gather this kind of thing is happening increasingly all over Rome. The large influx of foreigners and the preference of some well-off citizens for a luxury villa on the coast have both contributed to the change. The second of the two dwellings had in fact been divided into three apartments, one centering one the Greek-style garden at the back of the property, the other two — one rectangular, the other L-shaped and larger — around the Roman-style square hall at the front. For the second of these, the room facing the street had been transformed into a shop. It was this apartment that Aquila and Prisca had bought, for this arrangement enabled them to carry on their work as well as live in comfortable quarters. They got the best of both worlds, as they say.

As we came up to the house, we could see that the shopfront was closed, vertical wooden shutters sealing it off fully from passers-by. There was a small vestibule next to this which we entered off the street. A few steps inside it we came to the open door of the apartment. On it there was small sign

The apartment that Aquila and Prisca had bought.

with Aquila's name and trade. Since there was no-one about, Clement rapped on the door a few times — there was no doorknocker or ringer — to attract attention.

'Do you think we're early?' he asked Euodia.

'I don't think so,' she answered. 'We're probably just the first here.'

It wasn't long before someone appeared, a rather slim medium-sized man who bustled towards us. I'd been told in advance that he was Jewish but that didn't worry me. We Romans are a tolerant lot in such matters, and I'd got on fairly well with his race, though I'd never been to a meal in one of their homes. They don't entertain foreigners much. Something to do with their religious principles, I gather. They keep pretty much to themselves, even the expatriates. But this one, I gathered from a *An* conversation I'd had with Clement the other night, *unconventional* was an unconventional Jew in many ways, far more *Jew* liberal in his views.

'Because he's knocked about a bit in different parts of the Empire?' I'd asked.

'Not really,' he'd replied, 'though that might have something to do with it. More because he's adopted a new way of looking at the world which affects his outlook on such things.'

Well, then it had all come out! How Clement and Euodia had first become interested in this new way of looking at things in Corinth, through Aquila and Prisca. Clement said that he and Euodia got caught up in it themselves towards the end of their time there, and continued with it after they'd decided to move to Rome. They'd found it tough going here at first. Not that there is any lack of religious groups in Rome, each with their own shrine or temple, nor ample philosophical schools as well. But Clement and Euodia's outlook didn't seem to fit into either category. It was only when Aquila and Prisca reappeared on the scene that things brightened up for them. Just as they'd already done at Corinth and Ephesus, these two started regular meetings in their home. I've heard of private religious societies and philosophical dinners, though I've never had the doubtful privilege of attending either. Still, Clement told me this was quite different and Euodia went out of her way to assure me that I wouldn't feel out of place if I came along.

'Well, I'll take your word for it,' I said.

So there I was, a little nervous but curious all the same. I'd reasoned that my hosts were fairly level-headed types who wouldn't get mixed up in anything too out of the way. Mind you, being Greeks, they didn't have the advantage of a good Roman grounding in our religious and civic traditions, so they would be more inclined to fall for one of those secretive, emotionally-charged Eastern cults we've seen so much of lately. But then you wouldn't expect a Jew, however atypical, to get involved in that sort of thing, what with his race's over-refined moral scruples and stubborn addiction to a single god.

My hosts were fairly level-headed types.

When Aquila appeared, my friends didn't wait for him to come to the door, but went straight in to meet him. There was the usual arm-clasp and kiss between the men, though more

11

affectionate than is customary.

'Welcome, welcome, welcome,' said Aquila heartily. 'God's favour and peace be with you.'

'And with you,' returned Clement. 'It's good to be here again.'

Then, and this was most irregular, Aquila embraced Euodia as well, and exchanged kisses with her. You'd have thought they were brother and sister or something! I couldn't help wondering what our poet Martial would have made of it all: he found the habit of Roman men kissing one another on all possible occasions abhorrent enough and I was inclined to agree with him. Prisca then came into the room, dressed in a colourful, but simply decorated woollen gown. We had the same all around, though by now I was being introduced and greeted as well. With more propriety, I thankfully hasten to add.

Aquila embraced Euodia as well. This was most irregular.

'We're delighted you've come, Publius,' said Prisca, 'Clement and Euodia told us you might.'

Then, after depositing our cloaks with them, we took off our sandals and put on the slippers they provided. We also handed over the bunch of flowers and contribution to the meal which Euodia had prepared for us to bring.

We then fell to talking, Aquila drawing me out in quite fluent Greek about the itinerary of my recent trip, the weather on the sea-crossing from Achaia and the length of my stay in the city. In the course of the conversation, I discovered that as a young man he'd moved from Pontus to Rome, one of many thousands of immigrants from the Eastern provinces who had flooded the city in recent decades. Over a period of time he'd established a

13

thriving tent business, on the strength of which he'd married Prisca, a member of the well-known Acilia clan here. Unfortunately, they'd run into difficulty when Claudius suspected the Jews of stirring up political trouble and expelled them from the city. That's when Aquila and Prisca had settled in Corinth and, through their common business interests, met up with my friend. They'd moved around a bit more after that, to places like Ephesus and so on, and eventually, when the heat had died down in Rome, they decided to come back here and pick up where they'd left off. Being reasonably well off they'd managed to buy this modest apartment near the leather trade section, only a few streets away from their former friends.

The arrival of a large family

Just as I began to ask Aquila about his earlier days in Pontus, we were interrupted by the arrival of some other guests. It was a large family consisting of four children and an elderly grandmother, who had been living with her son and his wife since the death of her husband. Though I was introduced to them I couldn't remember all their names. They didn' live far away and the father, Philologus, was involved in bookselling, an associated leather trade. While the greetings continued, again with an excess of zeal to my way of thinking, I was able to take stock of the spacious square room in which we were standing. Now that the water system had apparently been improved in this part of the city, the small well in the centre — previously used to catch rainwater from the roof — had become ornamental only, and its sides were covered with potplants, giving the room a pleasant indoor garden appearance. A couple of bedrooms, presently drawn with curtains, opened off it. One was presumably a guest room since the host's children were married and had left home. I'd gathered from Euodia that Aquila and Prisca had quite a reputation for hospitality, putting up visitors for months at a time on occasions. It was pleasantly cool inside, refreshingly so after the mid-afternoon heat outdoors. It was also blissfully quiet in comparison with the chaos we had encountered on the streets outside.

I was drawn into conversation with the family which had entered. This went on for quite some time until two more guests arrived — a rather distinguished looking gentleman in an expensive-looking light robe and a companion in a simple tunic who could well have been his slave. Despite the obvious difference in rank between them, I was surprised, and a little shocked, at the lack of discrimination shown by Aquila and his wife in greeting them. The children immediately detached themselves from us and surrounded the slave.

'Lysias, Lysias,' they called.

'Well, well,' he said in mock horror. 'Don't tell me the barbarians have already invaded Rome!'

He was obviously a favourite with the youngsters and looked equally delighted to see them, tousling the boys' hair affectionately and complimenting the girls on their dresses. (They were wearing loose blouses over their ankle-length white stoles, while the boys had on the usual belted tunics appropriate to their age.) I was soon introduced to the slave's owner. Aristobulus was his name and he held down a relatively responsible post in the public service. We talked about his work for a while but had not got very far before Aquila clapped his hands and

Aquila and Prisca had a reputation for hospitality

15

called for our attention. He made one of those standard jokes about how is was easier to find agreement between two philosophers than between two water clocks. (I think Seneca started that one though perhaps he got it from somebody else.) He then went on to say that he'd just received word that the other guests were on the way, so we might as well move into the dining room in readiness for the meal. I took the opportunity to rejoin Clement and Euodia as we proceeded out of the hall.

'Is this when the meeting starts?'

'Is this when the meeting starts?' I asked Clement.

He looked at me quizzically, a slight smile playing around the corner of his mouth.

'It really began the moment we came into the house,' he replied, and left me to make of that what I could.

The dining room also ran off the main hall in which we'd been standing, and was of quite generous proportions. Aquila and Prisca had done well here too and I could see why the meetings were held at their place. You'd be hard put to fit the usual nine guests, including children, in Clement's flat. The original owner of Aquila's apartment had obviously agreed with Vitruvius' well-known dictum that a dining room should be twice the length of its width. This meant that two separate clusters of three couches around a table could be arranged in the room, giving space for up to eighteen adults and, where necessary, half-a-dozen children on benches or stools in the open space before the tables. As we entered, Prisca (or Priscilla

16

as everyone more familiarly called her) directed us to our places.

'Would you lie at the top end of the middle couch around the first table, Publius?' she asked.

I thought she must have been mistaken, for this was the place normally reserved for the most important guest.

'Here?' I said uncertainly as I reached the position.

She smiled and nodded, so I dutifully took my place. Beside me she positioned Clement and Euodia. Aristobulus, who by rights should have had my place, was seated to Euodia's left, along with his slave no less, on the couch for less important guests. I looked to see how he would take this double breach of etiquette, but he didn't seem to mind. If he did, he certainly kept his indignation well-hidden. At some of the meals I've been to, this would have been cause enough for him to walk out altogether. On the head couch opposite him Aquila took up his proper place on my right, with Prisca next to him. At the other end of the room, the second three-sided couch arrangement was open towards us so that we would all be able to see one another, though three of the children were sitting on folding stools in the middle. The mother, father and eldest boy took the couch to the left of these and the grandmother the head of the one opposite, next to the youngest girl. This left a number of spare places around both tables for the guests yet to come.

The place reserved for the most important guest.

Some of these now arrived. A Jewish weaver, his wife and two attractive daughters, greeted by one and all, joined the people at the other table. A few

17

steps behind them were two freedmen, and they filled up the remaining spaces at our table. All these placed their gifts on the tables before them alongside the others that our host had previously laid there. One of the freedmen, Gaius, was in the employ of a prestigious Roman family as a tutor to their children. He had actually been born in the household and, as so often happens these days, was later manumitted in recognition of his faithful service. At his ex-owner's request, though also at his own wishes, he'd stayed on in his previous job. Hermas, the other freedman, had been turned out by his former master and left to fend for himself. Since he had been unable to find work for months, it was only by relying on the government dole and the assistance of this little group that he had been able to survive. After introducing me to them and explaining their situation, Aquila rose and called for quiet.

Aquila called for quiet

'It's getting late,' he said, 'indeed the tenth hour is almost half gone, so I think we should begin the meal. It looks as if Felix has been kept back by his master again, so there's no telling when he'll arrive. Would you make sure, Philologus, that some food is left for him? Otherwise he'll probably miss out on a meal altogether. We all know what his master's like.'

Philologus nodded and delegated his eldest son to see that this was done.

Aristobulus' slave and the second of the two boys had accompanied Prisca out of the room shortly after we had entered and these now re-entered bearing the first course. The Jewish weaver's two daughters were also helping Prisca in the kitchen.

18

Before we began to eat, however, Aquila took up a cob of bread which his wife had laid on the table before him — homemade by the look of it, not brought from a bakery — and said he would like to give thanks. Some sort of offering to their god, I assumed. We Romans always reserve part of the food and drink for our household dieties and after the main course offer it to them for their acceptance. I'd heard that Jews did things differently, the start of the meal being signalled by the breaking of the loaf and some sort of prayer. What happened now was more like this. Instead of offering part of the bread to the god, Aquila reminded the people present that their god had offered something for them instead. His only son, no less, who died that they might live.

'Just before he sacrificed himself for us,' he went on to say, 'he took part in a meal with his followers just like the one we're having now. During this meal he shared around bread and told them that it represented him. Just as they needed bread in order to live physically, so, even more, they needed him if they were to experience real life. And so do we. This is why he wants us to continue having meals together and this is why we are meeting together today.'

Just how a dead person was going to do all this wasn't at all clear to me. But then Aquila went on to say that after this person was executed, he'd actually come to life again. I could hardly believe my ears, I can tell you, but that's exactly what he said! He'd gone to his father after death and this put him in a position where he could share his life with anyone who followed him, wherever they

Some sort of offering to their god, I assumed

19

were and no matter how many there were of them. A bit of him living in each of them, so to speak, or at least that's how I understood it.

'This means,' continued Aquila, 'that although he isn't physically with us in the room, he is nevertheless really present among us. As we eat the meal together, beginning with this bread' (which he was now breaking into substantial portions and passing among the guests) 'we'll experience him directly within ourselves, as well as through our fellowship with one another as we eat.'

He concluded all this with a brief prayer, if you could call it that. For it was made up on the spot so far as I could tell, and spoken in quite a normal voice. In it he thanked his god for all this and told him how much we looked forward to the meal and everything that went with it. Then he sat down to a chorus of 'yes', 'indeed', 'amen' and the like and began to eat.

Not ritualistic nor exotically mysterious

Well, this wasn't quite what I'd bargained for, I can tell you. Neither decently ritualistic nor exotically mysterious. All very simple and matter-of-fact really. I wondered what their god made of this slipshod and common way of doing things. It did seem to treat him rather casually. Not at all in the manner to which I would have thought a god was accustomed!

After we had been eating for a little while, Aquila turned to the grandmother and asked her a question.

'How are you managing, Mary, in this hot

21

weather we've been having? It's certainly unusual this early in the year.'

Clement confided in me: 'She's only recently come down to Rome from the hill-country in the far north, the original home of the entire family. Despite her fifty years, she's coped with the change well enough, but she's developed some sort of skin trouble which often causes her discomfort.'

She replied in her noticeably provincial dialect. 'Very much better, thank you Aquila, especially since last week when the whole group prayed for me.'

This led on to a discussion of the value or otherwise of certain medicinal creams and on the limited helpfulness of doctors generally. While this was in progress we began our first course. It was a small portion of the wheatmeal porridge which we normally eat in larger quantity as our main dish. It was garnished more than usual with a variety of relishes — at least mushrooms, olives and some herbs — and also flavoured with honey sweetening.

'This entree's extremely tasty,' I commented to Euodia.

'Priscilla's own recipe,' she explained. 'She won't tell a soul the exact mixture of ingredients she adds.'

I'll believe when I see with my own eyes

Then I was brought into the wider conversation and asked whether in my travels I'd heard anything about the great healing shrines in the East where so many miracle cures were supposed to take place.

'I've heard a lot of talk,' I offered, 'but much of it seemed far-fetched to me. I'll believe the sorts of thing I've been told about when I see them with my own eyes.'

A lively interchange then took place over the relationship between professional medical help and community prayer for healing. Some people's feelings were quite strong on the issue and for a moment or two it looked as if a real row would break out. But with a little help from Aquila it all settled down after a while and became far too subtle for me. I turned my attention to the first serving of wine that was about to be poured out by Aristobulus' slave.

It looked as if a real row would break out

The cups, like the dishes we'd been using, were made of earthenware, not the bronze and silver tableware you see in the very best of homes. Large spoons were provided for those remnants of the meal which our fingers couldn't handle. Also on the tables were bowls of water and serviettes, for washing the hands and cleaning the fingers before, during and after the meal. Often slaves see to this, with the help of sponges and even wine at times, but here it was a do-it-yourself arrangement. We had to keep the flies off ourselves, too. The wine itself, mixed with water rather than honey, was of reasonable quality and was delightfully cool to the palate. The children put pressure on Aristobulus' slave to pour them as much as their parents.

'Please, Lysias,' they urged.

'All right,' he responded, but only pretended to do what they asked.

Since the discussion about sickness had cooled down and everyone had finished their first course, Prisca got up to attend to the next one, followed by those who had helped her before. While this was happening Euodia broke in on the conversation.

23

'I've received a letter from Fortunatus this week,' she said, 'and he asks that his greetings be passed on to everyone.'

Fortunatus had apparently spent a short time in Rome with my friends some months before. During that time he had also attended the gatherings. He had now moved back to Miletus and was deeply involved with other believers there. Euodia read a few paragraphs from the letter in which he told of his latest doings.

A letter from Fortunatus

'Please pass on our warmest greetings in return,' said Aquila, 'and tell him we continue to pray for his welfare.'

Several others nodded their agreement.

When Prisca returned moments later, I could scarcely believe my good fortune. I'd been hoping for a little meat, so rarely had I eaten any lately. It was almost always in short supply and horribly expensive at the best of times. But here was a large plate of mixed meats for each table, and another with assorted vegetables. They must have been saving up all week for this, I thought. To my embarrassment, I was again served first. I took a little fish, turnips and beans, and then topped the lot off with a delicious smelling brine sauce. Across from me I was surprised to see Aristobulus place food on his servant's plate. Not only place it there, but exactly the same kind and amount as he had on his own plate. I've grown used to seeing even freedmen given inferior food and wine, and even different tableware than the more distinguished guests. But slaves generally ate outside the dining room. Now and again you hear of an owner who pursues a more liberal policy but it's still a rarity.

Slaves generally ate outside

Taking advantage of the momentary silence that occurred as we began to eat, Aristobulus said that Lysias had a problem that he would like to raise with the group at some point during the evening. Aquila indicated with his hand that he could go ahead now if he wished. He was just about to do so when there was the sound of sandals in the outer hall, a shuffle while they were taken off and exchanged for slippers, and then a young man — bearded rather than clean-shaven like most of us — appeared in the doorway.

'Welcome Felix,' said Aquila, motioning from his couch. Full of apologies the slave explained why he had been delayed.

Felix had been delayed

'My master sent me off on a wild goose chase across town,' he said, 'and it's taken up the entire afternoon.'

'Of course, of course,' said Aquila, 'we apologise for starting without you, but the evening was drawing on.'

Felix still hesitated at the door.

'Excuse me, Aquila, but would there be room for someone else at dinner as well?'

He beckoned with his hand and an even younger man, also bearded, stepped gingerly forward.

'This is Tyro,' Felix continued, 'A friend of mine whom you've heard me talk of before. I've spoken to him many times about the Lord. But last night when he was talking with Andronicus, that preacher who's in town at the moment, he suddenly knew that what he's so often heard was really true. He was baptised straight away in the Tiber [I shuddered at the thought: just think of its contents!] and then came around straight after work

Tyro was baptised in the Tiber — think of its contents!

27

to tell me what had happened. I felt sure you wouldn't mind if I brought him along.'

Aquila got up from his couch, went directly to the newcomer and embraced him.

'You're more than welcome here,' he said, 'more than welcome. We'll make up an extra place for you over there. It'll be a bit of a squeeze, but that's nothing, is it?'

Prisca was already bringing in some extra food from the kitchen.

'We'll let you get on with your meal,' she said, as they sat down. 'Plenty of time for questions afterwards. I'll just introduce you to the others here and you can begin.'

ow Lysias,' said Aquila, 'go ahead with what you were going to say.'

'Well it's a bit awkward really,' the slave replied, 'because it involves Aristobulus as well. But he's encouraged me to tell you about it. The problem is that Aristobulus wants to set me free. I'm genuinely grateful to him for his offer, but somehow I don't feel it's right. You see I'm convinced that God has called me to serve him and I think I can do that best the way things stand now. But he feels it would be better if I were free and sees no reason why that should affect things at all.'

Aristobulus wants to set Lysias free

Aristobulus agreed, enlarging on his reasons. Then, through various questions put to him and Lysias, the matter was explored further. In fact a discussion opened up on the question of manumission versus servitude generally and the two

freedmen had a good deal to say about the respect-
ive advantages and disadvantages involved. Clearly
it was no simple matter. While there could be certain personal and social advantages in becoming a
freedman, frequently there were real material losses
involved. Too many masters these days – Hermas'
was one of them – freed their slaves in order to rid
themselves of all responsibility for them. Others
made it a condition of their freedom that they continue to serve in the same post as before, but without the provision of housing or food that had
previously gone with it. The hovels some freedmen
had to live in were a disgrace, the wages inadequate
and their whole former family life disrupted. Some
were even worse off than day labourers who at
least could seek work where they wanted.

*Paul's letter to
their old church
at Corinth*

Gradually the discussion came back to the problem at issue. There were voices raised on both sides
and for some time the conversation went round
and round in circles.

'Didn't Paul have something to say about this?'
Prisca asked Aquila.

'That's right,' he replied. 'It was in one of his
letters to our old church at Corinth.'

'Can you remember which one?'

He pondered a moment.

'It's in the first one, I think, in the section where
he talks about marriage and the single life. You'll
find it in the chest in the bedroom with our other
papers if you don't mind fetching it.'

*Paul was an
old friend*

While she was out of the room, Aquila told me
that this Paul was an old friend of theirs who had
started groups all around the Empire and was at
present under house-arrest somewhere in the city,

awaiting trial on some trumped-up charge that had been levelled at him in Judaea. He had a special kind of wisdom in matters affecting their common life, and they often found it helpful to consult him personally about such things or go over what he had written. When Prisca returned, Aquila found the place in the scroll quite easily and read it out.

For the most part, Paul advised them to be content with their present state and not to change it. *Masters were really slaves* Those who were slaves should see it as an opportunity for serving others, for that's the basic responsibility we all have, whatever our station in life. Yet when the opportunity to become free arose, as it generally did, then they should not hesitate to become freedmen. For if anyone approached this new situation rightly, he would actually find new ways in which to help others. Then masters were told to remember that they were really slaves themselves, to Christ, and slaves, that they were really free in the area that mattered most.

This advice certainly turned the discussion in a more profitable direction and even gave me something to think about myself. Talk now revolved around the principle on which this Paul's judgement had been based. In what ways could Lysias' freedom enable him to serve Aristobulus more satisfactorily, or were there special circumstances associated with his case that meant it was an exception to this rule. Through all this Lysias himself, and others *Slaves were really free* who had supported his view, seemed to be coming around to a more positive attitude to Aristobulus' proposal. But clearly there were still things he wished to think about. He said so as he got up to help Prisca with the next course.

31

I n the short break that followed, Philologus informed the gathering that his eldest girl had prepared a small contribution for the meeting and would now like to present it to them. We often have such interludes during our dinners so I wasn't at all surprised at his proposal. There were muttered words of encouragement from all corners of the room as the little girl got up and moved to the wall so that she could see everybody.

'It's a song,' she said, 'one that I made up myself. It's about all the different sorts of things God has made.'

And then she sang, quite confidently, in a clear, true voice. We all clapped when she had finished, the other children loudest of course, and Aristobulus let out a sonorous 'Bravo!'. Prisca and the others, who had been waiting at the door not wishing to interrupt, then brought in the dessert. This contained a good choice of apples, grapes, pears and figs. After much washing of our fingers in the bowl and wiping on the serviettes to dry them, we each took our choice.

A song about things God made

As the conversation, almost for the first time, was being carried on in small groups (one near me was debating the ethics of chariot races in the stadium), I reflected on the degree of group involvement displayed by the people present. Often at meals I had attended, guests made use of their liberty during dinner to detach themselves from what was going on around them to write or dictate letters, transact business with a neighbour or sometimes just doze off between courses. I also noticed that members of this group were decently restrained in discarding their leftovers of food and drink on

the floor. There was a bit scattered around, but this had been done decorously and within acceptable limits, not in the ill-mannered way that you sometimes see.

Yet I couldn't help feeling that from a religious point of view the whole meeting left a lot to be desired. As far as I could tell, what had happened so far had contained scarcely anything religious at all. Why, they didn't even have a priest, let alone the ritual trappings that you expect. But perhaps there was more of a genuinely religious kind to come.

They didn't even have a priest

During this final course, I was able to talk to Aquila again and turn the conversation back to his time in Pontus. He spoke about his past experiences there and present contacts in the area and was able to answer many of the questions I put to him. But after a while someone else claimed his attention so I leaned across to talk with Aristobulus. It wasn't long before he launched into an account of how he'd become involved with this group. He'd experienced doubts for some time about the power of our traditional religion. Then, long impressed by the monotheistic emphasis of the Jews, and their moral outlook, he'd crept into a synagogue one day and found a genuine alternative. Not that he'd gone over completely to Judaism. Some of its dietary regulations and its — to my mind quite barbaric — practice of circumcision, prevented him from going the whole distance. He'd also kept quiet about his synagogue connection among his friends. His wife strongly disapproved but said nothing to anyone lest her social standing and political loyalty be called into question. After meeting Aquila and Prisca he'd linked up with this

Aristobulus impressed by the Jews

34

gathering instead. But although his slave had been persuaded to join, he'd failed to convince his wife that there was anything in it.

t this point we were interrupted by Lysias who, at Aquila's signal, had begun to refill the cups at our table. Felix was doing the same at the other. Aquila then took his cup in both hands and said:

'The wine that we've been drinking has been part of our meal and a help to our fellowship in the Lord. But it means more than this. For, as Jesus explained, it reminds us that he is the one who has created this bond through his death. It also stands as a promise to us of the fellowship we shall have one day with him when we sit down at his table and dine with him face to face. So as we drink this cup together, let us take these things to heart and be grateful for them, looking back with appreciation on the one and looking forward with anticipation to the other. And may our meetings express that oneness that we have with him more and more so that they are, as it were, a little taste of heaven on earth.'

In this spirit we all drank

In this spirit we all drank.

Since the meal was now virtually at an end, various guests were showing their appreciation of it with some hearty belches. Not wishing to be impolite, I naturally did the same. Prisca and Aquila looked suitably pleased at this expression of our enjoyment and acknowledged it with a slight nod.

As the children and slaves cleared away, and the guests got up to stretch their legs, Prisca checked

the oil supply in the saucer-shaped earthenware lamps on the tables and also made sure that the wicks were a reasonable length. Since dark was still a little way off, however, she did not light them immediately. Oil is too expensive to waste, as we are all well aware. The children had all gathered around Lysias who produced a game of draughts from somewhere and sat down in a far corner of the room. One of the older girls had also brought along her noughts and crosses set and the two boys began to play knucklebones. I wandered over and watched them for a while, absorbed as much as anything by the skill with which Lysias managed to lose while giving the appearance of so desperately wanting to win. Raucous shouts of joy greeted his defeat, only slightly tempered by parental hushes to be quieter.

Raucous shouts parental hushes

Meanwhile the guests were re-assembling themselves on the couches, though one or two took the opportunity to leave the room, presumably in search of the lavatory. This place might just be fortunate enough to share one on the ground floor with the occupants of the other apartment. As I went back to my couch, I began to wonder what would happen now that dinner was over. Normally this time is taken up with general conversation, the telling of jests or stories or the discussion of a moral topic or text, helped along with liberal servings of wine. Since our cups were being cleared away, I presumed that we weren't going to have any more of the latter. But beyond that I couldn't tell.

I made myself comfortable by leaning back against one of the cushions on the divan and easing my feet out of the slippers on to the cool mosaic floor. Normally you would expect terracotta or cement underfoot in a home of people with Aquila and Prisca's means. But thanks to its aristocratic origins, in this respect as well they had been fortunate. The room was undoubtedly a pleasant one. Spaced grill-windows, flanked by drapes, let in adequate lighting along one wall of the room. Several tapestries and wall-hangings decorated the white plaster walls. The motifs on these were fairly standard ones but had been quite well executed. The couches and tables were modest affairs. Instead of the beautifully-grained timbers and elaborately carved woodwork that you find in better class homes, here the low wooden tables had only those adjustable metal legs that are so popular these days and the headboards of the couches were quite simple in design. The fabric covering them was made from good, but not fine, material and the

The room was
a pleasant one

embroidery was workmanlike rather than extravagant.

Aquila asked
the spirit of his
god to guide

When everyone had seated themselves and Lysias had packed away the game, Aquila bowed his head slightly and asked the spirit of his god to guide all that now took place. As before he did this quite simply and matter-of-factly. After a short pause he then suggested we sing a song, the one the children particularly liked. This met with general approval. Gaius, who had a fine baritone voice, led off and soon everyone was joining in, the children clapping their hands as they sang. I even managed to join in myself after a while. I enjoy nothing more than a good sing but don't very often get the chance to indulge. We nearly lifted the rafters off in the last chorus, so goodness knows what the people next door made of it!

The song had no sooner finished than Clement closed his eyes and began to talk to his god. Like Aquila, he spoke in a quite ordinary fashion, almost as if his god were a close acquaintance in the same room. As Clement conversed with him, he repeated something that had been mentioned several times in the song, about the world as a present from the god to us. A strange idea, don't you think? He expanded on this at some length. He went into a lot of detail about so often taken-for-granted things that we use, see, hear and smell every day which come from god's hands. While he was talking, there were occasional murmurs of agreement from others in the room. At the end there was a loud affirmation from the whole group.

Clement spoke to his god in an ordinary fashion

This same pattern repeated itself as different people spoke, women as well as men, and even one of the children. Some of the conversations with the god were as long as Clement's, some no more than a few words. Most followed up in some way or other the subject which Clement had culled out of the first song. At one stage, for example, the Jewish weaver thanked the god for his generosity to his ancestors, listing a number of things which marked them out from other races, though also apologising for their constant failure to reciprocate. A very hesitant sentence or two also came from Tyro, in which he thanked the god that he now understood how much he had done for him, in particular the gift of his one and only son. At the

Men, women, children spoke

end of this, the heads of each family present, and one or two of the others, went across the room and laid hands on him, welcoming him into their community and pledging him their future support. He was actually moved to tears by this and could scarcely express his gratitude to them. Despite the strangeness of the occasion, I must admit to being a little moved myself. As they resumed their places Hermas said there was a psalm out of the sacred writings which he felt was particularly appropriate to the occasion. He must have had a good memory for this kind of thing, for the recitation lasted some minutes.

They laid hands on Tyro

'Would you like a copy of it?' he asked Tyro when he had ended. 'I could easily write one out for you.'

The other nodded, still a little overwhelmed, I think, by what had happened earlier and all the attention he was receiving.

During the slight pause that followed, Prisca got up and lit the lamps. By now it was almost completely dark outside and we could hardly see each other across the room. While she was doing this, Hermas began to tell a story out of the sacred Jewish writings. It was about one of the great heroes of the past, called David. From the way he talked they must have been hearing about a different part of his life each time they met. He certainly knew how to put across a story, I'll give him that, for I don't think there was one of us, adults as well as children, who made a sound while

Hermas' story about David

he was speaking. Another song followed, suggested this time by Aristobulus.

Then everyone settled back as Aquila began to speak. He started out by saying to them that the spirit of god now gave gifts in greater number than ever before, so much so that everyone received one or more of them. These gifts involved things we could say to one another or things we could do for one another. Some gave greater understanding of the god, of each other, of our outside responsibilities, or of the events going on around us. Some aided members personally with their problems or welded them together into a harmonious and cohesive group. Some assisted those in financial difficulties or dealt with other physical needs like sickness. Some helped people to communicate things to their god, or explain things communicated by others, which they felt so deeply that they could not put into ordinary words. All these were meant to be shared with others, not selfishly hoarded or only privately enjoyed. Together they provided the resources for growth, in every aspect of their lives, of each one present and the group as a whole. This was why it was important for everyone to discover what abilities they had been given, to discern when and how they should be exercised and to weigh carefully how much truth or just personal opinion the employment of others' gifts involved.

Aquila began to speak about gifts

'Above all,' he insisted, 'we must desire to exercise the most important gift of all, that of speaking God's word helpfully and relevantly to one another, and also seek to exhibit the most important quality there is, that of genuine loving care of one another.'

The most important gift of all

41

He concluded with a direct challenge to all those present to do this.

'Our whole welfare,' he pointed out gravely, both as individuals and as a group depends on it.'

It did not surprise me in the least that there was a short silence after he had finished. For while he had spoken without the usual rhetorical flourish that our popular moralists display, there was a force inherent in his words which could not be denied. I felt it myself, even though I did not fully understand all that he said. During this silence I noticed that the youngest child in Philologus' family had fallen asleep in her mother's arms and that the other daughter was leaning half-asleep against one of her brothers. A slight draught, slipping in through the drawn curtains, caused the lamps to flutter and the smoke coming up from the them curl lazily in the air. All around the walls gigantic shadows cast by our bodies contracted and expanded to the rhythm of the lights. Outside the rumble of heavy traffic entering the city after the daytime curfew was gradually increasing. It was just as well that the windows in this room faced inwards instead of out on to the street, and that the walls were solidly built. Otherwise it might have been difficult at times to hear what was being said.

Force without rhetoric in his words

The lamps flutter

The weaver's wife began to speak. 'As I was sitting here,' she began, 'thinking about what Aquila had said, I knew God wished me to say something, firstly to all of us, and then to one

particular person. God wants us to know that he will present us with more things to share with one another and that he will make the ones we experience now more helpful still. This will not happen if we concentrate on seeking the gifts themselves but simply as we concentrate on serving one another. If we're willing to do this we shall also find more scope for some of our gifts outside the group itself, among others we are hoping to influence for the Lord. In particular, God wants to assure you, Lysias, that this would be the outcome of the freedom Aristobulus wants to give you. It will not only enable you to serve Aristobulus in a greater variety of ways but also others in ways closed to you at present. So you are to go ahead and take this step with confidence.'

Lysias, you are to take this step with confidence

She stopped and, as you can imagine, given the previous discussion, the general response to this was very positive indeed. After a slight pause, Gaius stood up and walked across to Mary, the grandmother. Standing beside her, he placed his hand upon her head and called upon the others to pray with him for her. He then claimed on her behalf the god's power to heal, thanking him for the improvement that had taken place during the last week and asking that this might continue until she was fully well.

Gaius placed his hand on Mary's head

This seemed to be a cue for a whole assortment of prayers by different members of the group for various aspects of each others' lives. I must confess to growing a little sleepy as this went on, probably because of the smoke from the lamps as much as anything else, though some people did seem to me to go on at inordinate length in their prayers. I got the impression that Clement felt this at several points as well, for here and there he shuffled his slippers rather impatiently and sighed in a resigned manner. But eventually Aquila brought things to an end by suggesting that we sing together a little farewell song which everyone knew. We did so, and the meeting was over.

Well, perhaps not quite, for I remembered what Clement had said to me earlier about when it really began!

Philologus and his wife immediately bade good-night to their hosts and went out with their children, Prisca accompanying them. The second family, excusing their withdrawal by referring to the lateness of the hour, also made their farewells. Both groups came across to me on their way out and wished me a happy stay in Rome, and one of them invited me to an evening meal the following week. I accepted. The remainder stayed on, talking in small groups, and on her return Prisca offered them some more wine. I noticed Aristobulus discussing with Hermas in one corner of the room and confidentially giving him some money, overriding the other's protestations as he did so. The two slaves also said goodbye and Aquila conducted them through the hall to the main door We decided to take our leave as well and followed them out into the hall. Ahead of us Prisca had halted the two slaves just as they were about to leave and pressed two serviettes full of leftovers into their hands. They left and we began to make our own farewells. I thanked our host most warmly for including me in their invitation and they made it clear to me that I was welcome to come with Clement and

The meeting was over

We collected our cloaks and sandals

45

Euodia anytime during my stay in Rome. After receiving our sandals all but myself kissed one another goodbye, Aquila and Prisca commending them to the grace of god as they did so. Then we collected our cloaks, threw them over our shoulders and went out into the night.

Outside it was pitch black. Our capital's roads are only lighted on great occasions, so negotiating them at any other time is never easy. Except when the moon is reasonably full and fairly high in the sky. Apart from the two slaves, whom we could hear but not see in front of us, the street appeared to be deserted. Most people had been in bed for hours now, for we Romans tend to rise early and make the most of the light. Flickering lamps and smokefilled rooms at night are hardly conducive to staying up late.

'Felix,' called Clement to one of the slaves, 'I suggest we walk as far as we can together. It's safer that way.'

The others agreed and waited for us to catch up with them. At that moment Aristobulus also appeared through the doorway behind us.

Lysias has a torch

'I was hoping you wouldn't have gone too far,' he said. 'Lysias has a torch and if we go together we can all get the benefit from it. It'll be slightly longer for us, but that's no problem. We can look after ourselves if we have to, can't we Lysias?'

I can't say I was displeased at these suggestions. Rome is notorious for its night-time thieves and muggers. Not to speak of wild dogs, and even pigs,

running loose all over the place. In the narrow streets, when you can't properly see your way, the large wagons carrying freight in and out of the city after the daytime curfew can also be a danger to life and limb. Not that these were the only things you had to look out for. Too many people still emptied their slop-pails and toilet-pans out of their windows at night when nobody could see them. There was practically nothing you could do about it either. Whenever you went out at such a time, you just had to cross your fingers and hope for the best.

Cross your fingers and hope for the best

As we walked, and the others discussed among themselves the events of the night, I thought back over what had happened since we'd set out that afternoon. Although things had turned out very differently to what I had expected, by and large I had to say I'd enjoyed the evening. The people themselves certainly impressed me. That was one thing. And despite my misgivings about some of the proprieties they disregarded, beliefs they entertained and enthusiasms they gave reign to, there was something about their interchange, both during the meal and even after it, that strangely commended itself. There was something about their goings-on that was unmistakably real. Yet their meetings seemed to be grossly inadequate from a religious point of view, and the novelty of some of the things they did was most offputting. I wondered whether I would take up Aquila's and Prisca's invitation to attend the following week. It was hard to say. I wasn't sure at all. But I suspected I might.

If you are interested in knowing more about church life, or conferences on the Deeper Christian Life, you may write the publishers for more information.

Our Publications

The books listed below are available through your local Christian book store. The following prices are for the year of 1990 only. All books are paperback unless otherwise noted.

BOOKS BY GENE EDWARDS

BOOKS BY JEANNE GUYON

COMMENTARIES BY JEANNE GUYON

BOOKS BY OTHER AUTHORS

THE SEEDSOWERS
Christian Books Publishing House
P.O. Box 3368
Auburn, ME 04212-3368
207-783-4234